NATURAL WAYS TO IMPROVE TROUBLE VISION

Exploring the power of nature in vision correction.

By

Dr DOUGLAS JASON

Before this document is duplicated or reproduced in any manner, the publisher's consent must be gained.

Therefore, the contents within can neither be stored electronically, transferred, nor kept in a database. Neither in part nor in full can the document be copied, scanned, faxed, or retained without approval from the publisher or creator.

TABLE OF CONTENTS

ABOUT THE AUTHOR

INTRODUCTION

ABOUT THE AUTHOR

Dr DOUGLAS JASON is a certified dietician who has a strong passion for wellness and a big eagerness to help people all over the world. He uses healthy food, herbs, sauce and other useful tools to help mankind realized it's overall goal of optimum health.

TABLE OF CONTENTS

INTRODUCTION

If you detest wearing glasses and don't want to wear contact lenses, natural vision correction may be appealing to try. But there are no clinical trials to back up the idea that natural eyesight correction is effective.

Although natural vision correction techniques promise to reduce refractive problems in the eyes, they might not be effective.

Myopia (nearsightedness) and hypermetropia (farsightedness) are two refractive deficiencies of the eyes that are purported to be enhanced via natural concept modification techniques.

These techniques make use of eye workouts and massages to enhance or hone vision. However, while eye exercises might lessen the pressure on the eyes from gazing at screens all day, major eye conditions like glaucoma or macular degeneration need to be treated by a doctor.

In the quick-paced digital environment of today, many people are having visual problems. Maintaining excellent eyesight has become an increasing concern, whether it's due to extended exposure to screens, environmental concerns, or just the normal aging process. Some people look for natural alternatives to medical interventions like glasses, contact lenses, or surgery to enhance their vision. This writing examines several all-natural methods for improving visual health and offers information on food choices, eye workouts, and lifestyle changes that might improve eye function.

The following conditions are not helped by natural eyesight correction techniques:

Myopia

Presbyopia
Hypermetropia
Degeneration of the retina
Astigmatism

CHAPTER 1

WAYS TO CORRECT REFRACTIVE ERRORS.

prescribed eyewear
Since prescription glasses do not weaken the eye further or hasten the development of myopia or hypermetropia, they are the safest and most efficient technique of vision correction. A licensed optometrist should be consulted for prescription glasses.

To determine whether your refractive power has changed and whether you require new glasses if you have myopia, you should have your eyes examined annually. Myopia can progress quickly in youngsters, so they need to have their eyes checked by an ophthalmologist (eye doctor) every six months.

Utilizing contacts
Astigmatism, or an uneven corneal surface, can be treated with contact lenses to correct eyesight. People who don't want to wear glasses should consider them as an option. They shouldn't be worn more than six hours a day or past the time frame for which they were designed. They

must also be cleaned and stored according to instructions.

cataract surgery
In many instances, refractive surgery can help correct refractive problems. If you are a good candidate for surgery, an ophthalmologist can help you find out.

CHAPTER 2

TYPES OF REFRACTIVE SURGERIES

The cornea (transparent tissue layer over your iris) is converted into a thin, hinged flap during laser-assisted in situ keratomileusis (LASIK). To treat farsightedness, the cornea's contours are modified using a laser.

Epithelium, the cornea's outer protective layer, is cut with a laser during a procedure called a laser-assisted subepithelial keratectomy (LASEK). To repair the refractive error, the surgeon tries to alter the corneal curve.

Unlike LASEK surgery, photorefractive keratectomy (PRK) is a more intrusive treatment. The epithelium is taken out, and the cornea is then reshaped with a laser by the surgeon.

Can nearsightedness be cured by eye drops?

The FDA has not yet approved the use of any strength of atropine eye drops to treat myopia (nearsightedness). Trials, though, are being conducted under FDA oversight, and the outcomes so far are promising.

Atropine drops, given at a dose of 0.01%, have already been shown to delay the progression of myopia in children by roughly 50% in two significant trials carried out in Asia. Only kids between the ages of 6 and 12 can benefit from this method. For the effects of the medication to last, it must be taken as prescribed every night for at least 24 months. It is unknown if myopia will return if the drops are stopped.

Myopia cannot be cured, thus even after using atropine drops, children may still need to wear glasses or contact lenses. However, the condition might not worsen to pathological myopia or complicated myopia with the drops.

CHAPTER 3

NATIVE MEANS TO REDUCE EYE STRAIN.

Studies have indicated that exposure to some natural sunshine is good for the eyes, especially in young infants. Children who are exposed to outdoor light develop myopia more slowly than those who spend their time staring at devices, have less axial elongation, and have overall superior eyesight. However, between the hours of 10 am and 2 pm, it is best to avoid being outside in direct sunlight without sunglasses or UV protection for your eyes.

PALMING: Every four hours during the day, palming is a traditional eye exercise that is advised. Place your hands' palms over both of your closed eyes without applying pressure. Hold this position for about a minute while inhaling deeply. Your eyelid muscles will relax as a result of this activity.

Yawning and blinking: Less frequent blinking and screen exposure are common causes of dry, gritty eyes. Your tear glands may become active when you yawn, which may help with some eye strain symptoms. The discomfort can then be lessened by repeatedly blinking, which will spread the tears across your eyes. If it doesn't work, you can use eye gels or synthetic lubricants to keep your eyes moist.

Splashing cold water over your eyes can help relieve eye strain, especially if you've been staring at a computer screen for a while.

Rolling your eyes: Keep your back straight and slowly roll your eyeballs upward. After that, return them to their original positions.

Roll your eyes again, downward, sideways, and back. Every day, repeat. This straightforward technique can ease eye strain and pain.

The 20-20-20 rule states that when using a computer, you should look away from it for 20 feet for 20 seconds every 20 minutes. You can avoid headaches and eye strain because of this.

The muscles that sharpen your acuity (muscles of accommodation) can be relaxed by staring out the window for at least 20 minutes each day.

Take breaks from your screens by avoiding them on the weekends. Turn off all of your electronic devices at least four hours before bedtime. To prevent eye tiredness, make sure to take breaks from your job every hour.

Aim straight forward while receiving a brow massage. Apply light pressure to your brows with your fingertips. Gently rub the area beneath your eyes as you move down the edges of your eyeballs. Next, apply pressure to the junction of your upper and lower eyelids. Three times a day, repeat. Use clean hands, and avoid applying too much pressure.

Figure 8: Pay attention to a spot on the floor that is about 8 feet distant. Your eyes should now move in a figure-8 pattern. After 8–30 seconds, trace the fictitious figure in the opposite direction.

Change your way of life by giving up smoking, drinking less alcohol, and eating more foods high in antioxidants. Consume colorful veggies (bell peppers, eggplants, carrots, and greens) and fruits (bananas, berries, almonds). Ensure that diabetes, high blood pressure, and other diseases are under good control.

Sidebar is open

Natural Improvement of Vision.

CONCLUSIONS

Maintaining a high quality of life requires taking care of our vision. There are natural approaches to improve impaired vision, in addition to medical procedures, which are often helpful. Individuals can support their visual health and possibly stop the advancement of some eye problems by adopting a holistic strategy that includes dietary changes, lifestyle adjustments, and workouts for the eyes. However, it's necessary to keep in mind that natural remedies might not provide magical outcomes overnight and that speaking with an eye care specialist is essential for an appropriate diagnosis and recommendations. We can make great progress toward clearer and healthier eyesight by implementing these organic techniques into our regular routines.